DISABILITY AND THE DISABLED-ISSUES, LAWS AND PROGRAMS

LIFE SKILLS INSTRUCTION IN A TIME OF ACCOUNTABILITY

DISABILITY AND THE DISABLED-ISSUES, LAWS AND PROGRAMS

Additional books in this series can be found on Nova's website under the Series tab.

Additional E-books in this series can be found on Nova's website under the E-book tab.

DISABILITY AND THE DISABLED-ISSUES, LAWS AND PROGRAMS

LIFE SKILLS INSTRUCTION IN A TIME OF ACCOUNTABILITY

BETH ACKERMAN
AND
KATHERINE QUIGLEY

Nova Science Publishers, Inc.
New York

For permission to use material from this book please contact us:
Telephone 631-231-7269; Fax 631-231-8175
Web Site: http://www.novapublishers.com

LIBRARY OF CONGRESS CATALOGING-IN-PUBLICATION DATA

Ackerman, Beth.
Life skills instruction in a time of accountability / Beth Ackerman and Katherine Quigley.
p. cm.
Includes index.
ISBN 978-1-61668-780-9 (softcover)
1. Students with disabilities--Education--United States. 2. Special education teachers--Training of. 3. Educational accountability--United States. 4. School improvement programs--United States. 5. United States. No Child Left Behind Act of 2001. I. Quigley, Katherine. II. Title.
LC4815.A28 2010
371.9'04482--dc22

2010016070

Published by Nova Science Publishers, Inc. † New York

CONTENTS

Chapter 1

INTRODUCTION

Currently the *No Child Left Behind* (NCLB, 2002) federal legislation mandates that students with disabilities receive instruction in the core curriculum classes of English, math, science, and social studies, and that Adequate Yearly Progress in these courses be maintained by all schools. In addition, public schools are responsible for assessing students with special needs at the same intervals as their regular education peers. "Alternate assessments are relatively new in most states, developed for students who were not included in most large-scale assessments until Federal law mandated their participation" (National Center on Educational Outcomes, 2005, p. 1). As a result, students with intellectual disabilities must be assessed in the four core curriculum areas. The implementation of these alternate assessments provides the government with accurate statistics regarding the success of students. As a result, this academic curriculum does not always reflect the social needs of students with intellectual disabilities. According to Agran, Alper, & Wehmeyer (2002):

> There is an intentional narrowing of the curriculum. When the narrowing is combined with high-stakes testing procedures established to ensure accountability, the result too often is that the 'general curriculum' focuses only on core academic content areas, to the exclusion of other areas that might be just as (or more) important to students with significant disabilities (p. 124).

It has become increasingly evident that students with severe cognitive delays require a curriculum that incorporates functional academics, daily living, occupational, and social skills training. "Special education must resist the constant push for an academic curriculum emphasis rather than the more important career/life skills approach that their students will need for successful community living and working" (Brolin, 1997, p. 7). A life skills curriculum supported by academics allows for students with intellectual disabilities to learn how to utilize skills that enable them to live and work as independently as possible, as well as remain in compliance with federal legislation.

Chapter 2

BACKGROUND OF THE STUDY

The manner in which students with disabilities have been educated has varied greatly throughout history. This was evident when reviewing the history of special education, pertinent legislation, the manner in which students with intellectual disabilities are educated, and the need for specific curriculum and social skills training. Throughout the 1800s and the turn of the 20th century, children with disabilities were placed in institutions from an early age. This was where they resided throughout their lifetime, receiving little instruction. This trend began to change in the 1880s and 1890s with the beginnings of deinstitutionalization of those people with mild handicaps (Lawrence, 1999).

Chapter 3

LEGISLATION

In 1954 with *Brown v. Topeka Board of Education*, the law stated that education was an equal right to all students. The debate of integration culminated with the passage of federal legislation in 1974 titled the *Education for All Handicapped Children Act*, which is now titled the *Individuals with Disabilities Education Act* (IDEA). The act mandated that "students with disabilities be provided an appropriate education designed to meet their need in the least restrictive environment (LRE)" (Kavale, 2000, p. 4). In addition, the concept of mainstreaming was introduced with Public Law 94-142 as schools were now required to place children with disabilities with their nondisabled peers to the maximum extent possible. "Depending upon a student's functioning level and the structure of the school system, the student may either be in an integrated setting with non-disabled peers or a segregated environment with other disabled students" (DeWeaver & Kropf, 1992, p. 38).

Another key legislative action was Section 504 of the *Rehabilitation Act of 1973* (Section 504). This civil rights law served as a protection of rights entitled to students with disabilities. "Section 504 requires entities receiving federal funds (e.g., schools, colleges) to make 'reasonable accommodations to known physical or mental limitations of an otherwise qualified handicapped (person)'" (Shriner, 2000, p. 232).

The *Americans with Disabilities Act of 1990* (ADA) only served as a reinforcement of the principles found within Section 504. The ADA reiterated that the primary focus should remain on making individual decisions regarding reasonable modifications on policies, procedures, and practices. *Goals 2000: Educate America Act of 1994* (Goals 2000) and the *Improving America's*

Schools Act of 1994 (IASA) provided a framework for the requirement of setting performance goals and standards.

Current legislation entitled *No Child Left Behind* "continues the legacy of the *Brown v. Topeka Board of Education* decision by creating an educational system that is more inclusive, responsive, and fair" (Paige, 2004, p. 13). This has had a tremendous impact on the education of students with intellectual disabilities. Historically, legislation has worked to provide accommodations as well as access to general education classes and the curriculum. The 1997 amendments to IDEA specify that "students with disabilities have access to and progress in the general education curriculum" (Wehmeyer et al, 2002, p. 157).

Chapter 4

SOCIAL SKILLS

The curriculum for students with disabilities can easily be divided into the areas of academic and nonacademic skills. Social skills instruction would be considered nonacademic sklls. "Traditionally, the emphasis on social skills has been overshadowed by academics. However, many educators acknowledge the need for an increased emphasis on social skills development to promote greater social competency for students with high-incidence disabilities" (Kolb & Hanley-Maxwell, 2003, p. 163).

Similar to other skills, social skills instruction must be deliberate and skills must be learned and practiced within the various natural settings and the environments that they will occur (St. Peter, Ayres, Meyer, Park-Lee, 1989). Students with intellectual disabilities can learn to get along with others and adjust to various social situations when taught these social skills. According to the American Association for Intellectual Disabilities (AAID), "impairments in adaptive behavior can seriously limit an individual's opportunities in work situations, living arrangements, and leisure activities" (Thomas, 1996, p. 349).

Chapter 5

EDUCATION OF STUDENTS WITH DISABILITIES

There are two concepts that are essential to understanding the education of students with intellectual disabilities: intelligence and adaptive behavior. The construct of intelligence refers to the general mental capabilities. According to the 9th edition of Mental Retardation: Definition, Classification, and Systems of Supports, significantly sub-average intellectual functioning was "defined as an IQ of approximately 70 to 75 or below" (Cuskelly, 2004, p. 118).

The second essential concept to be aware of is adaptive behavior. "It now consists of three areas, as resulting from factor analytical research studies" (de Bildt, Serra, Luteijn, Kraijer, Sytema, & Minderaa, 2005, p. 318). These areas are conceptual, social, and practical skills that enable students to function independently. These conceptual skills include reading and expressive language, reading and writing, money concepts, and self-directions. Furthermore, social skills included interpersonal relationships, responsibility, self-esteem, and following rules and laws. Finally, the practical skills are defined as personal hygiene and grooming, daily living activities, and occupational skills (AAMR, 2002).

The awareness of these two concepts enabled an educator to have a thorough understanding of intellectual disabilities. In order to meet the needs of the students in special education, specific skills in these deficit areas must be taught. Due to recent changes in legislation, research-based curriculum specifically designed for students with intellectual disabilities is emerging. As a result, nonacademic skills such as daily living, social, and occupational skills are not receiving enough attention (Brolin, 1997).

This study sought to analyze this relationship by determining if students participating in a curriculum focusing on personal-social skills achieved significantly higher scores on the Knowledge Battery and Competency Rating Scale (CRS) than students who did not participate in the program.

Chapter 6

STATEMENT OF THE PROBLEM

According to Ford, Schnorr, Meyer, Davern, Black, & Dempsey (1989):

> We know that many of the curricular offerings in today's schools (e.g., language arts, math, science, social studies, physical education, and fine arts) can accommodate these new students when adaptations are planned and instructional supports are made available. But further examination reveals that the existing scope of schools' curricula is not broad enough to encompass all the activities or areas of competence that may be appropriate for a given student (p. 3).

It is essential to expose students with intellectual disabilities to personal or social skills. The development of independence, self-confidence, socially acceptable behavior, and maintenance of friendships were among the essential social skills necessary for students to learn in order to function within their community (Brolin, 1997).

Chapter 7

Hypothesis

Students in classes that utilized the Life Centered Career Education's (LCCE) Personal-Social Skills program achieved significantly higher scores on the Knowledge Battery (KB) and Competency Rating Scale (CRS) than students who did not participate in the program.

Literature Review

It was important to recognize the need for students with intellectual disabilities to be exposed to a curriculum that was both academic and functional in order for students to learn essential social skills. This was accomplished by reviewing the historical developments, legislative progress, and curriculum developments.

Chapter 8

HISTORICAL REVIEW

A chronological review indicated that the manner in which students with disabilities have been viewed and educated had varied greatly. According to *Mental Retardation* (Payne & Patton, 1981), the historical perspectives regarding the attitudes and treatment of individuals with intellectual disabilities can be divided into nine distinct periods. The first era, prior to 1700, was considered a state of confusion. Since there was a limited knowledge base, the attitudes about and the treatment and perceptions of people with mental deficiencies varied greatly. There was no consensus among Western societies as to who should be treated and why and how they should be treated. As a result, different patterns of treatment developed reflecting a time of confusion. If any service was provided, it would typically be nourishment and housing.

Following this era was the Awakening, from 1700 to 1800, which created two key concepts that impacted people with intellectual disabilities. The first was a new social attitude; "it held that all 'men'- even those who were exceptional – had rights" (Payne & Patton, 1981, p. 6). As a result of this attitude, the second implication would be that the attitudes and time were conducive for idealistic people to develop their philosophies of Humanism.

According to Payne & Patton (1981) the era of "Early Optimism" occurred from 1800 to 1860 and was illustrated through the enthusiasm towards working with people with disabilities. In addition, the birth of special education occurred in Europe with the work of John Marc Itard (1774-1838). He developed five major objectives to help overcome metal problems. However, this optimism and belief that people with intellectual disabilities could be cured were later replaced by the pessimism in the fourth period of

Disillusionment occurring between 1860 and 1890. People with intellectual disabilities was now being perceived as incurable.

This period of disillusionment led to the "Sounding the Alarm" period. Between 1890 and 1930 the institutions that were originally designed to train individuals with intellectual disabilities were now assuming the role of caregiver. More dramatically, the change in social attitudes toward the population of people with intellectual disabilities was detrimental. In 1964 Kanner wrote, "The mental defectives were viewed as a menace to civilization, incorrigible at home, burdens to the school, sexually promiscuous, breeders of feebleminded offspring, victims and spreaders of poverty, degeneracy, crime, and disease. Consequently, there was a cry for the segregation of all mental defectives, with the aim of purifying society, of erecting a solid wall between it and its contaminators" (Payne & Patton, 1981, p.13).

Following this era, the progress in the treatment was simply put "On Hold" between 1930 and 1950. However, views were slowly changing with the realization of several key concepts regarding the scientific research on the causes of intellectual disabilities. These changes in views in the causes of intellectual disabilities led to the time referred to as "A Turning Point" occurring between 1950 and 1960 (Payne & Patton, 1981). This quiet revolution was marked by the formation of the National Association for Retarded Children (NARC) in 1950. This organization served as lobbyist, service provider, and advocate for research for people with intellectual disabilities. In addition to the establishment of the NARC, social and political views were shifting from fear and repulsion to tolerance and compassion.

From 1960 to 1970 special education began to take "Center Stage." National attention was placed on people with intellectual disabilities as President Kennedy had a sister with intellectual disabilities. He established a President's Panel to serve as a guide and source for national policy which led to the establishment of what is now the Office for Special Education and Rehabilitative Services. Consequently, the Civil Rights Movement was extended to people with disabilities (Payne & Patton, 1981).

Finally, the era "From Action to Introspection" occurred from 1970 to the 1980s, when it was established that people with intellectual disabilities have personal and civil rights, guaranteeing services and protection which must be extended to the educational setting. The historical changes in this time period were a result of the numerous legal rulings that occurred.

Throughout history the terminology of special education has undergone continuous changes. The vocabulary most often chosen to describe people with cognitive limitations has been historically "mental retardation"and more recently "intellectual disabilities" is the term that is being used. *IDEA* used the term "disability" which is "probably an unfortunate choice of terms because it conflicts with current philosophy in special education and with the intent of the *IDEA* by focusing on a person's lack of ability" (Thomas, 1996, p. 5). This term has slowly begun to be viewed as unacceptable just as its predecessors: mental deficient, idiot, imbecile, and moron. The National Association for Retarded Children chose to change its name to "the Arc" eliminating any reference to retardation by eliminating the acronym. Likewise, in 2002 the Council for Exceptional Children's Division on Mental retardation voted to change the name to The Division on Developmental Disabilities (Hourcade, 2002).

Chapter 9

LEGISLATION

Beginning in 1954 with *Brown v. Topeka Board of Education*, the law stated that education was an equal right to all students. Following this groundbreaking case, two key pieces of civil rights legislation have had an impact on education: Section 504 of the Rehabilitation Act of 1973 and the Americans with Disabilities Act (ADA). Since these two pieces of legislation were civil rights acts, it was mandatory for schools to adhere to these laws.

The first of these legislative actions was Section 504 of the *Rehabilitation Act of 1973*. Section 504 prohibited the discrimination against individuals who meet the definitions of a disability. According to Wegner (1988), Congress's primary objective was to "honor the requirements of 'simple justice' by ensuring that federal funds not be expended in a discriminatory fashion" (Smith, 2001, p. 336). This civil rights law served as a protection of rights entitled to students with disabilities. "Section 504 requires entities receiving federal funds (e.g., schools, colleges) to make 'reasonable accommodations to known physical or mental limitations of an otherwise qualified handicapped (person)'" (Shriner, 2000, p. 234).

Section 504 strived to provide students with disabilities an equal opportunity to gain the same benefits from school and to reach the same level of achievement as their nondisabled peers. It is important to note that Section 504 applies only to entities that obtain federal subsidies. On the other hand, the *Americans with Disabilities Act of 1990* (ADA) applies to most entities, regardless of whether they receive federal funds. The ADA served as a reinforcement of the principles found within Section 504 and reiterated that the primary focus should remain on making individual decisions regarding reasonable modifications on policies, procedures, and practices. "The ADA was intended as companion legislation to the *IDEA* and Section 504 of the Rehabilitation Act of 1973. The most comprehensive civil rights legislation enacted since the 1960s, the ADA expands the prohibition of discrimination against people with disabilities to the area of employment, transportation, communications, and public accommodations and reinforces rights guaranteed in earlier pieces of legislation" (Rea & Davis-Dorsey, 2004, p. 66).

The ADA contained several titles which corresponded to various aspects of discrimination for people with disabilities. Title I focused on discrimination within the work place. Title II dealt with state and local governmental entities such as prohibiting discrimination within schools. Finally, Title III focused on public accommodations such as within stores, hotels, and restaurants. According to the ADA, all entities were required to make reasonable accommodations and modifications to guarantee that people with disabilities had access to goods and services. In the educational setting, the ADA had produced numerous positive results such as "a more diverse workforce; increased accessibility of opportunities, activities, and facilities; increased labor resources; a refreshing call for innovation, creativity, and flexibility; and a new recognition and appreciation of the strengths, contributions, and abilities of people with disabilities" (Rea & Davis-Dorsey, 2004, p. 69).

The definition of a disability under Section 504 and the ADA contained three main criteria (Rehabilitation Act & sec; 706[8]):

1 has a physical or mental impairment that substantially limits one or more of such person's major life activities,
2 has a record of such impairment, or
3 is regarded as having such impairment (Smith, 2001, p. 338).

There were two requirements detailed in Section 504 and the ADA which affected students: nondiscrimination and free, appropriate public education (FAPE). The nondiscrimination policy referred to the concept that the students with disabilities should be allowed to participate in activities that were available for all students. This would include the same academic curriculum, nonacademic extracurricular activities, health services, recreational activities, athletics, student employment, clubs, specific courses, and field trips. It is essential to understand that students must meet the "otherwise qualified" criterion as stated in IDEA. "This means that a person with a disability must be qualified to do something before the presence of a disability can be a factor in discrimination" (Smith, 2001, p. 340).

In addition to nondiscrimination, Section 504 and ADA required that schools provided students with disabilities with a FAPE. This would include the provisions that were designed to meet the individual educational needs of students with disabilities comparable to that of the needs of the nondisabled students. A FAPE must be provided regardless of the nature and severity of the disability. Students must have nondiscriminatory evaluations and placement. Furthermore, procedural safeguards enables parents to contribute significantly in decisions concerning the evaluation and placement of their students. Finally, students must be integrated with their nondisabled peers to the maximum scope possible, a trend referred to as mainstreaming.

In addition to Section 504 and ADA, the concept of mainstreaming was enforced with Public Law 94-142 as schools were now required to place children with disabilities with their nondisabled peers to the maximum extent possible. "Depending upon a student's functioning level and the structure of the school system, the student may be in either an integrated setting with nondisabled peers or a segregated environment with other disabled students" (DeWeaver & Kropf, 1992, p. 38).

The debate of integration culminated with the passage of federal legislation in 1974 entitled the *Education for All Handicapped Children Act*. This law was revised and reauthorized as the *Individuals with Disabilities Education Act (IDEA)* of 1997. *IDEA* mandated that students with disabilities be provided an education planned to meet their needs in the least restrictive environment. The placement of students with disabilities is one of the most important decisions agreed upon by the IEP team. Likewise, it can be a controversial area resulting in many due process hearings (Yell & Katsiyannis, 2004, p. 29).

The two essential principles of *IDEA* were the FAPE and providing these services within the students' LRE. This legislation details that support for special education and related services to children be provided in a variety of settings such as child care, preschool, elementary, middle, and high school. According to *IDEA* this is accomplished through the development of Individual Education Programs (IEPs) that provide students with disabilities with a free, appropriate education in a minimally-restrictive environment. This must be provided for students, age three to 21, who have been found eligible for services. This document was considered the cornerstone of the *IDEA* as a means of providing students with a FAPE (Gartin & Murdick, 2005).

IDEA was a federal programmatic mandate that governed all special education services and therefore provided funding for students identified as eligible. On the other hand, Section 504 was a civil rights statute; therefore, no funding was provided to assist in compliance. The criteria for determining identification, eligibility, appropriate education, least restrictive environment, and due process were all different between *IDEA* and *Section 504*.

The major differences center on the flexibility of the procedures. There were less specific criteria for students found eligible under Section 504. Therefore, schools may offer less assistance and monitoring. Students found eligible for services under *IDEA* must meet specific criteria as well as the degree of regulation was more specific with regards to timeframes, parental participation, and paperwork requirements. Furthermore, *IDEA* made provisions for students with disabilities from ages 3 to 21, while Section 504 covered people with disabilities throughout their lifespan. In addition, *IDEA* focused on the educational needs of people with disabilities, while Section 504 covered a variety of aspects of people's lives such as employment, public access, transportation, as well as their educational needs (deBettencourt, 2002).

The 2004 *IDEA* reauthorization (*IDEA 2004*) made provision for many positive changes. According to the Council for Exceptional Children (2006), the most important of these changes include:

- Guaranteed that students with disabilities participate in accountability systems.
- Reduced the paperwork burden.
- Established methods to decrease the number of students from culturally and linguistically diverse backgrounds inappropriately placed in special education.
- Ensured the discipline provisions for students with disabilities continue to protect the rights of students to a free, appropriate public education.
- Provided funding for professional development for special educators.

The most current legislation entitled *No Child Left Behind* is "the 21st century iteration of this first major foray into education policy" (Paige, 2004, p. 13). This has had a tremendous impact on the education of students with intellectual disabilities. Previously, legislation had worked to provide accommodations as well as access to general education classes and the curriculum. The 1997 amendments to *IDEA* specify that "students with disabilities have access to and progress in the general education curriculum" (Wehmeyer et al, 2002, p. 158).

It is also important to review the legislation specific to working with students who are mentally retarded. The first landmark case was *Diana v. State Board of Education* (1970) which required the state of California to correct assessment procedures. Three important results of this case were that students must be tested in their primary language, culturally unfair items must be eliminated from test and assessments, and intelligence tests must be developed to reflect Mexican-American culture (NASET, 2006).

Later in 1984 *Larry P v. Riles* similar results indicated California was discriminating against students who were mentally retarded by using IQ tests as the assessment measure for eligibility. *Wyatt v Stickney* (1972) directed that children with intellectual disabilities in state institutions had the right to treatment. *PARC v Commonwealth of PA* (1972) would play a fundamental role in future federal special education laws. This legislation assured that schools could not exclude students with intellectual disabilities and that these students must be provided with a free public education. Furthermore, it called for deinstitutionalization due to inhumane conditions (Black & Salas, 2001). Similarly, *Mills v Board of Education of DC* (1972) provided guidelines for a free public education and due process. In addition, it was mandated that special education services must be provided despite the school's financial capability (NASET, 2006).

Chapter 10

CURRICULUM

Historically, curriculum planning began with the passage of PL 94-142 when schools became responsible for the education of students with intellectual disabilities and IEPs drove the curriculum. Barnes and Barnes (1989) described guidelines for the development of a curriculum specifically designed for students with intellectual disabilities. The major goal was to identify what needed to be taught, by moving them toward independence in adulthood. Goals and objectives should be developed in the areas of academic, recreational, prevocational and vocational, social and emotional, and life skills. The key is to strike a balance between students being left in academic classes and functional life skills (Sutton, 1993).

The curriculum for students with intellectual disabilities should be driven by the specific needs of individual students, rather than their label, current issues, or the general education curriculum (Thomas, 1996). However, recent changes in legislation have created shifts in philosophical views and have directly impacted curriculum planning. "As societal perspectives change, so does the focus of school curriculum. One of the strongest current influences on curriculum is the school accountability movement" (Ahlgrim-Delzell, Algozzine, Browder, Flowers, Karvonen, & Spooner, 2004, p. 1).

Instruction for students with intellectual disabilities was at one time characterized by a developmental approach to teaching. Students with disabilities were often asked to complete repeated drill and practice on isolated skills that were not easily transferable to the general community. Since students with disabilities typically take a longer time to acquire a skill, they were often focusing on similar skills throughout their education without progressing. As a result, educators found that students were completing their education with the skills associated with younger children rather than adults made ready to enter the community (Ford, 2001). Therefore, specific instruction should be provided in functional academic skills that will be used in everyday life. "As these individuals move to secondary education settings, the curriculum should take on a stronger career preparation and life skills emphasis" (Hourcade, 2002, p. 4).

Current educational trends and legislation allows for students with intellectual disabilities to receive special education services in an environment which provided access to the general education curriculum. "The State shall have such academic standards for all public elementary school and secondary school children, including children served under this part, in subjects determined by the State, but including mathematics, reading or language arts, and (beginning in 2005-2006 school year) science, which shall include the same knowledge, skills, and levels of achievement expected of all children" (CEC, 2003, p. 7). This mandated that students with disabilities take part in a curriculum appropriate for their age and grade level.

In addition to participating in the general education curriculum, students must demonstrate that they have made progress in this curriculum. Adequate yearly progress (AYP) is a controlling measurement to determine accountability towards each student's achievement (CEC, 2001). Since schools are now mandated to maintain AYP in the areas of mathematics, reading or language arts, and science, students with intellectual disabilities must be exposed to a curriculum that contained these subjects.

"Over the past 30 years there has been a significant shift in the focus of the curriculum for students with significant cognitive disabilities. As a field we have moved from a developmental model to a functional life skills model to one that promotes access to the general education curriculum" (VDOE, 2006-2007, p.7). However, as students with cognitive disabilities progress through school, a focus should be placed on the maturation of functional academic skills. Educators must find a balance between providing the students access to the general education curriculum and providing instruction in a functional curriculum. As students advanced to secondary education settings, a career preparatory and life skills emphasis is placed on curriculum and instructional matters (Hourcade, 2002).

Finding a curriculum that allows students with mental disabilities to be exposed to the general education curriculum, while receiving instruction in these vital areas continues to be of utmost importance. *IDEA* mandated that the curricula used within special education classes be research-based and peer-reviewed (Cernosia, 2005). In addition, "In education, national policies such as

No Child Left Behind (NCLB) require that teachers use scientifically proven practice in their classrooms" (Odom, Brantlinger, Gersten, Horner, Thompson, & Harris, 2005, p. 137). NCLB requires that all students be assessed in reading, math, social studies, and science, which was contradictory to the functional approach typical of how skills were acquired for students with disabilities (Browder & Cooper-Duffy, 2003).

The concept of a life skills curriculum has been increasing in awareness and practice. According to the 1989 text *Best Practices in Mild Mental Retardation* (Robinson, et. al.) curriculum options were discussed and, "although there are a number of curricular options, we believe that the one best suited for a vast majority of students with mild intellectual disabilities is one based on the principles inherent in the life skills/adult outcomes approach" (p. 25). In 1994, Smith and Hilton determined that the curriculum should be driven by the needs of the students rather than by clinical labels, philosophical issues, or the initiatives occurring with regular education (Thomas, 1997).

Syracuse Community - Referenced Curriculum Guide

Within the field of disabilities two leading life and vocational curriculums are the Syracuse Community-Referenced Curriculum Guide for Students with Moderate and Severe Disabilities and the Life Centered Career Education program. Both of these curriculums tie assessment and lesson planning together (Moon, 2000). The Syracuse Curriculum Guide was based on the premise that, "every student, no matter how severe his or her disabilities, is capable of living, working, and recreating in the community" (Ford, Schnorr, Meyer, Davern, Black, & Dempsey, 1989, p. 3).

The Community-Referenced Curriculum Guide focused on the community living domains of self-management/home living, vocational, recreational/leisure, and community functioning. In addition functional academic skills like reading, writing, money handling, and time management were addressed. Furthermore, the embedded social, communication, and motor skills were concentrated on throughout instruction in all of the content areas. This would include interacting positively with peers, using vocalizations and symbol systems, and moving about in the environment effectively. All of these areas were targeted as they would allow students to function in the real world.

The Syracuse Community-Referenced Curriculum Guide addressed the concern for educators of how to integrate life skills into an academic curriculum. It is proposed that this curriculum be used as one part of the numerous other course offerings available. If the content areas cannot be met in regular education classes, an alternate method would be to incorporate the content area into informal parts of the day, natural learning times, or recess and free time.

The community living domains of self-management/home living, vocational, recreational/leisure, and community functioning were all areas where students must receive this consistent deliberate instruction. The self management/home living realm encompasses skills that were essential to everyday functioning. "These types of skills are common in people's daily lives and present frequent opportunities to make personal choices (e.g., what to eat, when to do something). By not teaching students to participate in such common and regular daily routines, we may seriously restrict their opportunities to influence decisions about their personal lives (Ford, Schnorr, Meyer, Davern, Black, & Dempsey, 1989). The six major goal areas include eating and food preparation, grooming and dressing, hygiene and toileting, safety and health, assisting and taking care of others, and budgeting and planning/scheduling.

According to the Syracuse Guide, vocational skills were essential in helping to establish a positive self-image, gain the respect of others, and make contributions to the community. The vocational domain covered three major goal areas: classroom/school jobs, neighborhood jobs, and actual community jobs. These settings represent a variety of integrated environments and build the students' vocational resumes (Ford, Schnorr, Meyer, Davern, Black, & Dempsey, 1989).

The recreational/leisure skills domain was centered on increasing the life skills of a person with disabilities. This would include five major goals areas: school and extracurricular, activities to do alone, activities to do with family and friends at home, activities to do with friends in the community, and activities that increase one's physical fitness (Ford, Schnorr, Meyer, Davern, Black, & Dempsey, 1989).

Finally, general community functioning was based on the fact that learning can take place in various settings. "Meaningful instruction is not limited to school settings; it can also take place in the surrounding community where students can learn and practice skills in real-life settings" (Ford, Schnorr, Meyer, Davern, Black, & Dempsey, 1989, p. 77). One cannot assume that students with intellectual disabilities will acquire these skills based on exposure alone. Educators must provide instruction in order for students to receive consistent and repeated opportunities to develop these skills.

In addition to the community living domains, The Syracuse Community-Referenced Curriculum Guide stressed the instruction of embedded skills. These skills included communication, motor, and social skills. These skills were reinforced throughout all aspects of instruction in a variety of content areas. With regard to social skills, there are 11 social skill functions identified. "No cookbook approach to social skills instruction could meet the widely varied needs of students with moderate and severe disabilities. Rather, we have provided some guidelines for thinking about social skills in general as well as for planning specific social skills programs." (Ford, Schnorr, Meyer, Davern, Black, & Dempsey, 1989, p. 184).

Chapter 11

LIFE CENTERED CAREER EDUCATION

The LCCE curriculum was based on the premise that career education is more than just a part of an educational program--it should be the major focus of a program. Career education began in the early 1970s as educators became aware of the need to refocus their instruction on specific skills that benefited students in their adult life. The concept of career education focused on the facilitation of growth and development for all roles in life, settings, and events. These roles were defined as "a productive and independent family member, citizen, employee, and participant in a variety of avocational/leisure activities such as recreational pursuits and hobbies" (Brolin, 1997, p.17). Furthermore, emphasis is made that educational experiences should be community-based to provide students with events in a variety of settings.

"Research during the past three decades clearly revealed that students must learn four major categories of skills: academic, daily living, personal-social, and occupational" (Brolin, 1997, p. 9). The LCCE placed its emphasis on three domains: daily living skills, occupational skills, and personal-social skills. "This is not to imply that career education is the only education students should receive, but it should be a significant and pervasive part of what is taught" (Brolin, 1997, p. 9).

LCCE was chosen as the curriculum for the purposes of this study due to the integration of academics with life skills training as well as the assessment instruments available. The LCCE curriculum contained a set of curriculum-based assessment instruments designed to measure the Daily Living Skills, Personal-Social Skills, and Occupational Guidance and Preparation. This curriculum focused on career education for regular and special education students. These competencies were identified as targeted areas based upon research, input from previous studies, and professional opinions (Brolin, 1997). Each competency was then classified under one of the three major curriculum areas referred to as domains.

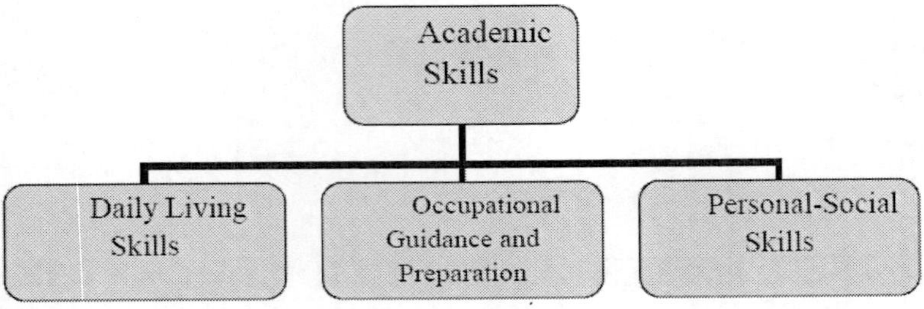

Chart 1. LCCE Curriculum Domains (Brolin, 1997, p. 13).

The Daily Living Skills domain contained competencies that were essential goals for students in special education to reach their most independent level possible. These targeted competencies included managing personal finances, selecting and managing a household, caring for personal needs, raising children and meeting marriage responsibilities, buying, preparing, and consuming food, buying and caring for clothing, exhibiting responsible citizenship, using recreational facilities and leisure time, and getting around the community (mobility).

An additional domain targeted would be that of Occupational Guidance and Preparation. In an effort to help students attain their highest potential, students must be exposed to a variety of aspects related to vocational awareness. Addressing students' need to become aware of the diverse job possibilities available to them accomplishes this objective. In addition, students were helped to develop the necessary skills, participate in a variety of work experiences, and learn to make logical and viable job choices. The competencies that were designated to address occupational curriculum are knowing and exploring occupational possibilities, selecting and planning occupational choices, exhibiting appropriate work habits and behaviors, seeking, securing, and maintaining employment, exhibiting sufficient physical-manual skills, and obtaining a specific occupational skill.

The third domain was the Personal-Social competency area and served as the curriculum utilized within this study. The Personal-Social competency focused on the independence, self-confidence, socially acceptable behavior, and maintenance of friendships for the students with intellectual disabilities participating within the study. The primary competencies that were included in instruction were achieving self-awareness, acquiring self-confidence, achieving socially responsible behavior, maintaining good interpersonal skills, achieving independence, achieving problem-solving skills, and communicating with others. The following are LCCEs Domains.

LCCE's Personal-Social Domain

Achieving Self-Awareness

1. Identify Physical and Physiological Needs

- List basic physical needs
- Identify ways to meet physical needs
- List basic psychological needs
- Identify ways to meet psychological needs

2. Identify Interests and Abilities

- Identify abilities common to most people
- Identify interests common to most people
- Demonstrate goal setting in relation to pursing an interest or ability and show how goals are attained

3. Identify Emotions

- Identify common emotions (fear, love, hate, sadness)
- List ways in which one's emotions affect the behavior of self and others
- Identify ways in which one may cope with emotions
- Differentiate particular emotions in self and others

4. Demonstrate Knowledge of Physical Self

- Identify major systems of the body
- List personal physical characteristics
- Describe physical characteristics and dimensions
- Identify major parts of the body

2. Acquiring Self-Confidence

1. Express Feelings of Self-Worth

- List positive physical and psychological attributes
- Express ways in which positive attributes make him/her feel good
- List the characteristics necessary to feel good about oneself
- Describe ways in which the actions of others affect one's feelings of self-worth

2. Describe Others' Perception of Self

- List potential reactions of others to oneself
- Construct a personal view of how others see oneself
- Describe the relationship between one's own behaviors and others' reactions
- Demonstrate awareness of individual differences in others

3. Accept and Give Praise

- Identify statements of praise in everyday activities
- List appropriate and inappropriate responses to praise
- Respond to praise statements by others
- List the effects of praise on oneself

4. Accept and give criticism

- Identify critical and/or rejecting types of statements
- List appropriate ways to respond to criticism and/or rejection
- Respond appropriately to critical statements
- List positive and negative effects of criticism

5. Develop confidence in oneself

- Identify and describe positive characteristics of oneself in a variety of areas
- List appropriate ways to express confidence in oneself
- Make positive statements about oneself

- Identify potential reactions of others to expressions of self-confidence

3: Achieving Socially Responsible Behavior

1. Demonstrate respect for the rights and properties of others

- Identify personal and property rights of others
- Identify reasons for respecting the rights and properties of others
- Demonstrate respect for others and their property
- List appropriate situations and procedures for borrowing the property of others

2. Recognize authority and follow instructions

- Identify common authority roles
- Identify aspects of following instructions
- Identify situation in which the individual has the right to disregard instructions from authorities

3. Demonstrate appropriate behavior in public places

- Identify appropriate behavior in public places
- Identify and demonstrate appropriate behaviors when using transportation facilities
- Identify and demonstrate appropriate behaviors when using eating facilities
- Identify and demonstrate appropriate behaviors when using recreational facilities

4. Know important character traits

- Identify own acceptable character traits
- Identify acceptable character traits in others
- List character traits necessary for acceptance in group activities
- List character traits that inhibit acceptance

5. Recognize personal roles

- Identify current roles

- Identify possible future roles
- List roles of significant others
- Describe the rights and obligations in personal roles as they interact with the roles of others

4: Maintaining Good Interpersonal Skills

1. Demonstrate listening and responding skills

- Identify proper listening and responding techniques
- Identify positive outcomes of listening and responding appropriately
- Identify negative aspects of listening and responding inappropriately

2. Establish and maintain close relationships

- Identify qualities of an individual who would be desirable in the dating process
- Identify and demonstrate appropriate procedures for making a date
- List activities that are appropriate for a date
- Identify characteristics of close relationships
- List different types of close relationships
- Recognize and respond to intimate feelings of others
- Identify persons with whom one could establish a close relationship

3. Make and maintain friendships

- Identify necessary components for a friendship
- List personal considerations in choosing a friend
- List rights and responsibilities important in personal friendships
- List activities that can be shared with friends

5: Achieving Independence

1. Strive towards self-actualization

- Identify important characteristics for personal growth
- List elements necessary for a satisfactory personal life
- Identify sources for continued educational/psychological growth

2. Demonstrate self-organization

- Develop plan of daily activities
- Identify areas of responsibility in personal life
- Identify reasons for organizing one's responsibilities/activities
- Develop ways in which personal organization relates to greater independence

3. Demonstrate awareness of how one's behavior affects others

- List ways in which behavior affects others around us
- List appropriate behaviors for a variety of situations
- List different cues elicited by others that behavior is inappropriate
- List ways to correct inappropriate behavior

6: Making Adequate Decisions

1. Locate and utilize sources of assistance

- Identify situations in which one would need advice
- List available resources for resolving problems
- Given particular situations, describe the procedures for contacting persons for assistance
- List potential outcomes of seeking advice

2. Anticipate consequences

- Describe consequences or outcomes of decision-making
- List and demonstrate knowledge of ways in which personal behavior produces consequences
- Describe the concept of maximum gain for minimum risk

3. Develop and evaluate alternatives

- Define the meaning of alternatives
- List possible alternatives with respect to a personal goal
- Describe a compromise with respect to a personal goal
- List resources for information that develops alternatives

4. Recognize nature of a problem

- Given a list of situations with positive/negative aspects of personal ideas, examine each as a positive or negative
- Identify why ideas, values, and plans have both potentially positive and negative implications
- Identify a situation which requires examination of positive/negative aspects

5. Develop goal-seeking behavior

- Identify ways that goals affect one's life
- List outcomes to be considered in goal setting
- List examples of individuals who have set and attained their goals
- Set one goal for school, home, recreation
- Set short-term and long-term personal goals
- Identify characteristics of realistic goals
- Identify appropriate persons for obtaining assistance with setting and achieving goals
- Identify potential barriers to goals
- Set model personal goals

7: Communicating with Others

1. Recognize and respond to emergency situations

- Identify sights and sounds of emergency situations
- Identify appropriate authorities to contact in emergency situations
- Describe personal communication indicating emergency situations
- List personal responsibilities in emergency situations

2. Communicate with understanding

- Demonstrate a variety of verbal expressions related to communication
- Identify and demonstrate methods of speaking appropriately in a social conversation
- Demonstrate proper use of telephone
- Demonstrate appropriate volume and intensity in conversation

3. Know subtleties of communication

- Identify nonverbal elements of communication
- Identify verbal expressions that correspond to feelings
- Identify verbal expressions that are consistent with feelings
- Demonstrate verbal and nonverbal elements of communication (Brolin, 1997, pp. 69-104).

Chapter 12

SOCIAL SKILLS

Social skills training was typically an integral aspect of programs for people with intellectual disabilities. It was essential that students initiate and maintain positive social relationships with their family, peers, teachers, and people within their community. "Social skills are often defined as a complex set of skills that include communication, problem-solving and decision-making, assertion, peer and group interactions, and self-management" (Kolb & Hanley-Maxwell, 2003, p. 163).

Social skills are both observable and measurable behaviors that promoted independence, acceptability, and a good quality of life. "These skills are crucial to adjustments and normal functioning, and deficits have been closely linked to psychopathology and behavior problems" (Matson, Mayville, Lott, Bielecki, & Logan, 2003, p. 58). The research on intellectual disabilities indicated that social skills were of utmost importance in the quality of life and adjustment of people with intellectual disabilities into their community and vocation. "Numerous studies have proven that the lack of appropriate social skills is a major factor contributing to the failure of persons with intellectual disabilities in community placements" (Paraschiv & Oiley, 1999, p.3).

According to Barnes and Barnes (1989) educators have four major goals when teaching social skills. The first is to support students in learning how to read social cues and develop suitable responding behaviors. Secondly, it is essential to provide opportunities to socialize and practice these skills. Next educators must take on the role of educating others regarding the unique social needs of students with intellectual disabilities. Finally, it is essential to provide direct instruction on these specific social skills (Sutton, 1993). Similarly, Bertone, Boyle, Mitchel, & Smith (1999) stated that social skills goals can be met by incorporating direct instruction, structuring a positive classroom environment, and implementing cooperative learning strategies and activities.

In a historical review of special education, social deficits were identified early as detrimental to the development of students with intellectual disabilities. However, there were few instances of social skills training. In the 1950s authorities on disabilities indicated that social competency was most affected by the experiences within school. As students were integrated into regular education classrooms, poor social skills contributed to the fact that students with disabilities were frustrated with failure. This resulted in students being placed in separate classes to create a non-threatening classroom environment. “The less threatening academic atmosphere would ensure success experiences resulting in enhanced self-concept and decreases in showing off, teasing, and stealing other children’s things that were believed to be part of the youngsters’ with mild mental retardation behavioral repertories” (Robinson et al, 1989, p.271).

One of the earliest social skills training programs was the Social Learning Curriculum (Goldstein, 1974) developed by the Curriculum Research and Development Center in Mental Retardation at Yeshiva University. This was a social education curriculum directly geared toward addressing social interaction skills and providing information to students regarding their community and the daily living environment. Since the development of that curriculum, special education service delivery models changed focus and attempted to program for students with disabilities in the least restrictive environment (Robinson et al, 1989).

According to Taylor & Larson (1999) specific social skills training during adolescence can be effective in positively influencing students’ behavior (Kolb & Hanley-Maxwell, 2003). Despite this research, there was little consensus within current curricula regarding what the content of social skills training should include. “Social incompetence can lead to failure cycles and eventual poor school and adult outcomes” (Cartledge & Kiarie, 2001, p. 40). Despite this fact, there was little evidence that social skills were being systematically taught.

Chapter 13

ETHICAL CONSIDERATIONS IN SPECIAL EDUCATION RESEARCH

In 1969 the AAMR(America Association of Mental Retardation) adopted ten general principles when performing research on students with intellectual disabilities. The first principle centered on the fact that all research must conform to the same scientific, legal, and moral principles which justify all research. Secondly, all research with human subjects must be performed by qualified individuals. Furthermore, the research can only be carried out if the benefits of the objective outweighed the potential risk to the participants. The fourth principle reflected the fact that caution should not be limited to physical harm but should preclude psychological damage to the subjects as well as to their families (AAMR, 2006).

The fifth ethical principle to be implemented was that coercion of students is prohibited. In addition, compensation must be provided for any unusual inconvenience resulting from the study. It is also important to understand that all ethical aspects in the experimentation with people who were mentally retarded is clearly stated and that consent must be obtained if there is any risk or if one's identity may be revealed. The ninth principle centered on the premise that experimentation should be planned in a manner in which pain, suffering, and inconvenience was avoided. Finally, it was the researcher's responsibility to report the findings to the scientific community (AAMR, 2006).

Since qualitative research was empirical, it relied on factual information as well as observations and direct experiences. When completing the LCCE's Competency Rating Scale (CRS) forms, it was essential to be aware of the ethical standards that related to qualitative research. It was essential to recognize standards of high-quality work and to avoid or expose unethical behavior. "Qualitative field research, like all behavior, must follow the four cardinal virtues of antiquity: prudence, justice, wisdom, and courage" (Bruckerhoff, 1996, p. 2).

It was suggested that qualitative research was about human relationships. In order to establish an appropriate relationship between the researcher and the persons being studied, the researcher must have an interest in the people being studied, listen well, show respect, keep accurate records, be honest regarding intentions of the study, exercise caution, do no harm, and report the limitations of the study (Bruckerhoff, 1996).

Theoretical Review

Typically social skills are defined as the ability to get along with others and the exhibition of character traits. The concept of social skill acquisition relates to the theory of Emotional Intelligence described by Daniel Goleman (1997). "Emotional intelligence is the ability to access and interpret a given situation accurately and to manage oneself to relate effectively with others" (Kolb & Hanley-Maxwell, 2003, p.170). The five distinct dimensions found within emotional intelligence were self-awareness, managing emotions or self-control, motivation, recognizing emotions in others, and handling relationships. Research indicated that a person's emotional intelligence was more predictive of achievement within school and the workplace than IQ. "Children need to learn to manage their feelings appropriately, interact effectively with others, and motivate themselves if they are to be productive students and or workers" (Menta, 2006, p.1).

In addition, Albert Bandura's Social Leaning theory can be applied to the social skills development of students with intellectual disabilities. Social learning emphasized the importance of the observation and subsequent modeling of behaviors, attitudes, and emotional reactions of others. This theory was based on the premise that social interactions play a fundamental role in the development of cognition. "Bandura's social cognitive theory posits that behavior change is a function of setting goals based on outcome expectations associated with the behavior change, the tasks required to achieve those goals, and self-efficacy expectations for achieving the goals" (Heller & Rimmer, 2006, p. 1).

The Social Learning theory can easily be applied to the education of students with intellectual disabilities. "Social learning theory explains human behavior in terms of continuous reciprocal interaction between cognitive, behavioral, and environmental influences" (Kearsley, 2006, p.1). Bandura's theory also sets the theoretical framework for behavior modification techniques. These techniques were frequently used within special education classrooms to help achieve desired behaviors. As the social learning theory dictated, the LCCE curriculum focused on blending academics, daily living, personal-social, and occupational skills through social interactions within a variety of instructional settings (Brolin, 1997).

Chapter 14

METHODOLOGY

No Child Left Behind mandates that students with intellectual disabilities have access to core curriculum courses. The life skills program, Life Centered Career Education (LCCE), was integrated into the curriculum of high school students with intellectual disabilities. The LCCE program was chosen as it integrated essential academic instruction along with Personal-Social skills, Daily Living skills, and Occupational Knowledge lessons.

The study determined improvements made in the social skills of students pre- and posttest scores of the LCCE Knowledge Battery and Competency Rating Scale (CRS). Observations in the differences between the control group and an experimental group were made. Therefore, the hypothesis was that students in classes that utilized the LCCE's Personal-Social Skills program achieved significantly higher scores on the Knowledge Battery and Competency Rating Scale (CRS) than students who did not participate in the program.

PROCEDURES

The study began with the four educators participating being trained on the administration of the Knowledge Battery (Form A) and CRS. This was accomplished by each educator being provided with the introductory material that described the instrument and gave guidelines for test administration, detailed instructions to students, and scoring information along with templates for scoring and student recording forms. All educators began by administering the pretest evaluation. The LCCE Knowledge Battery determined the initial level of each student's Personal-Social skills.

The two special education teachers participating in the experimental instruction of the 39 subjects were trained on the LCCE program. The LCCE curriculum was administered to the selected 19 subjects over the course of seven weeks. Each week focused on one competency of the LCCE's Personal-Social curriculum:

- Week 1: Competency 10: Achieving Self-Awareness
- Week 2: Competency 11: Acquiring Self-Confidence
- Week 3: Competency 12: Achieving Socially Responsible Behavior
- Week 4: Competency 13: Maintaining Good Interpersonal Skills
- Week 5: Competency 14: Achieving Independence
- Week 6: Competency 15: : Making Adequate Decisions
- Week 7: Competency 16: Communicating with Others

The competencies addressed each week contained three specific sections for educators to apply. These sections included objectives, activities or strategies, and the role of adults in helping students achieve the identified goals. The teachers were provided with identical lesson plans and materials. Following the completion of the LCCE program, all four of the educators administered the equivalent, Form B, of the Knowledge Battery and reevaluated the students using the CRS, to determine the effectiveness of the intervention. Finally, a LCCE survey was administered to the educators involved in the study in order to provide additional information regarding any improvements that occurred in the study.

This experiment was classified as a nonequivalent control group, pretest/posttest design. This can be illustrated as administering a pretest to determine the dependent variable (Y_1) to the experimental and control group, applying the experimental treatment or independent variable (X), and the administration of a posttest to both groups that once again measured the dependent variable (Y_2). This was classified as nonequivalent since the student selection was based upon the students school.

SAMPLE

The students were placed either into the LCCE class for seven weeks or continued to receive instruction from the current curriculum. The schools

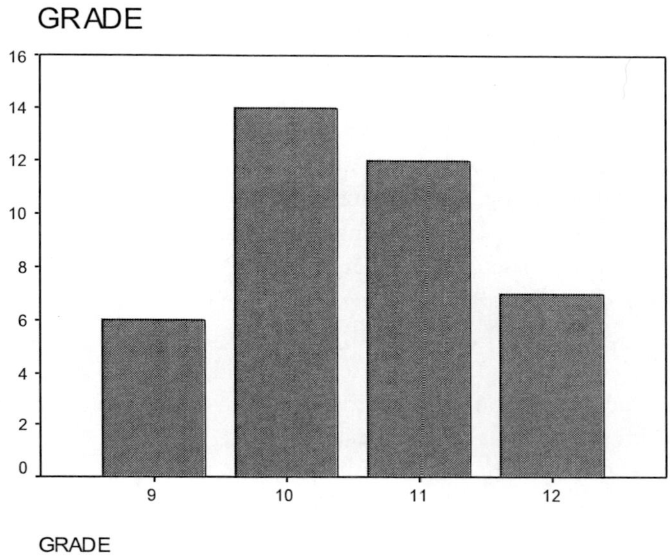

Graph 3. Frequency of Grade.

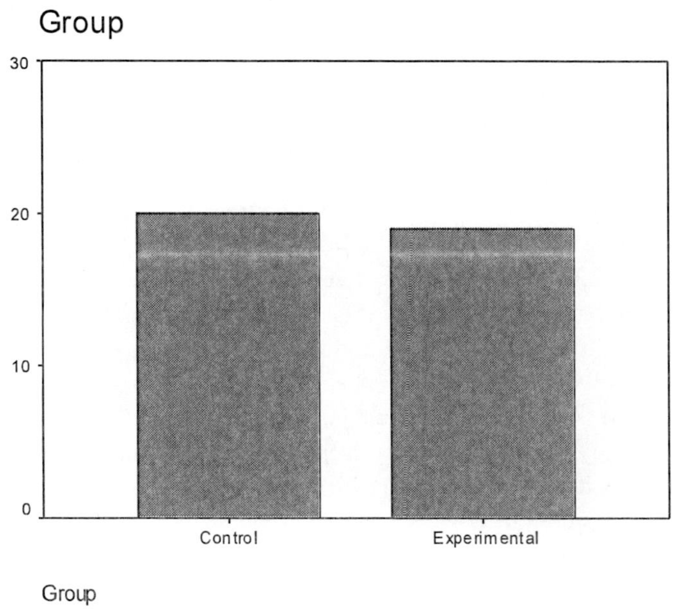

Graph 4. Frequency of Control and Experimental groups.

INSTRUMENTS

The LCCE Battery of assessment tested the students' general knowledge of the 21 competencies as well as their ability to demonstrate the desired competencies. The Knowledge Battery was broken into the three LCCE domains: Daily Living, Occupational Knowledge, and Personal-Social. In order to assess student improvement, educators administered the LCCE's Knowledge Battery specifically related to the Personal-Social competencies.

The Knowledge Battery was a standardized criterion-referenced instrument consisting of 200 multiple choice questions covering all of the curriculum domains, 21 competencies, and 97 sub-competencies. The Personal-Social portion contained questions for each of the targeted competencies with a total of 70 questions.

The Knowledge Battery's main purpose was to assess the knowledge important to functioning as a family member, an employee, a productive citizen, and in meaningful vocational activities (Brolin, 1997). This curriculum-based instrument field tested specifically for students with mild intellectual disabilities. In addition to the Knowledge Battery, the LCCE's Competency Rating Scale (CRS) also sought to identify strengths and weaknesses and determine the effectiveness of instructional strategies within the special education classroom.

Statistical analysis indicated the Kuder Richardson formula (KR 20) was utilized to determine reliability of each test, domain, and the total battery. Results indicated that the reference group scored one standard deviation below the mastery level, which was 17 out of 20 items. This translated into the fact that this battery was useful in the identification of student instructional needs and that there was not any test that was either too easy or too difficult. In addition, the KR 20s ranged between .55 and .82 with a median score of .72. The total battery on the KR 20 was .98, indicating that "the stability of the tests and total battery were also found to be good" (Brolin, 1997, p. 126). For the domain of Personal-Social skills, the Pre KR 20 score was .95, Post KR score was .96, and Test/Retest was .90, all indicating that the items have a high correlation to the domain they represent. Final measures of reliability, determined using the Pearson product moment correlations, ranged from .58 to.83 with a median of .745; for the total battery the correlation was .94. This indicated that the items correlate strongly with their respective domains (Brolin, 1997).

The LCCE Knowledge Battery demonstrated construct, content, and criterion-related validity. The construct validity was discerned on the basis of several projects from the Office of Special Education Programs through the US Department of Education and a federal special education project called the Competency Assessment Inventory Project (CAI). This allowed the LCCE curriculum to be developed with the input of special education teachers, as well as other educators. "The result was a competency-based curriculum which purported to cover all critical career/life skills that needed to be taught to mildly handicapped students (K-12)" (Brolin, 1997, p.119).

The content validity of the LCCE was addressed in numerous ways. This was accomplished through item writers developing questions that spanned the range of instructional objectives. Next, the administrators of tests evaluated test items through the utilization of field tests and agreed upon the appropriateness and status of items within the test. Finally, nine experts were given a field test with the task of analyzing each item to determine what competency they believed the questions addressed. Results indicated that the Personal-Social domain questions most often fell outside their domain. It was determined that "many of the items were written using a daily living or vocational example" (Brolin, 1997, p.127).

Criterion-related validity was performed in field tests as well as teacher judgments of the mastery, partial mastery, or non-mastery for each competency. This was completed in order to provide an external criterion against which the student was compared. Correlations between the actual scores and the teacher ratings were also made with a "Pearson product moment correlations revealed significant correlations at the .05 level for 17 out of 20 competencies" (Brolin, 1997, p.128).

The Personal-Social skills correlations score of .80 indicated a high level of correlation between the two Personal-Social skill tests. "Equivalency correlations between Form A and Form B are approximately equal when comparing pretest and retest" (Brolin, 1997, p. 130).

In addition to these quantitative methods, the use was utilized through an observational scale and educator survey. The LCCE's Competency Rating Scale (CRS) was completed along with the pretests and posttests. The CRS was a means of "providing educators with a systematic means of assessing student mastery of the subcompetencies" (Brolin, 1997, p. 151). Furthermore, the CRS can be employed to determine individual strengths and weaknesses, evaluation and development, and curriculum planning.

Since the CRS required subjective judgments to be made, it was essential that raters used the same criteria when completing the assessment. The CRS provided four ratings for student performance based upon the educators' observations, personal records or notes, and written or verbal reports from other personnel. Students were considered: Not Competent, Partially Competent, Competent, or Not Rated.

The educators completed the CRS for the Personal-Social domain. Following the completion of each CRS, the student's total actual score (TAS), which was the sum of all ratings, was determined. The actual score (AS) per item was then calculated by dividing the TAS by the number of items rated (N). The AS was then employed to evaluate progress made between pretests and posttests.

In addition, the educators completed the Communication Styles Checklist and the Curriculum Content Checklist developed by the CEC (Council for Exceptional Children) to be used in conjunction with the LCCE. These checklists were utilized to provide additional information regarding the rationale behind the results. The checklists were originally designed to help educators promote awareness of individual differences. "The checklists give teachers a tool to determine areas in which individual and cultural differences can be promoted, as well as areas that can be improved" (Brolin, 1995, p. ix).

Chapter 15

DATA ANALYSIS

The means of the experimental and control groups were compared utilizing the statistical technique of Analysis of Covariance (ANCOVA). The ANCOVA procedure examined the inequalities among group means, taking into account the influence of a covariate. By comparing the means for the two groups, experimental and control, the linear associations between the posttest and pretest were given.

RESULTS OF THE STUDY

It has become increasingly apparent that students with severe cognitive delays required a curriculum that integrated functional academics, daily living, occupational, and social skills training. A functional curriculum supported by academics allows for students with intellectual disabilities to utilize functional skills that enabled them to live and work within their community. However, the current trend is for students to be exposed to the general education curriculum, preventing students from receiving essential instruction in nonacademic areas such as personal-social skills. The Life Centered Career Education (LCCE) curriculum was a viable option for educating students with cognitive delays in an integrated life skills and academic curriculum.

Chapter 16

DATA ORGANIZATION

The descriptive statistics were compared with respect to each student's scores on the LCCE Knowledge Battery and CRS pretests and posttests. By utilizing the standard scores on the Knowledge Battery and CRS, the mean and standard deviation were determined and utilized for comparison.

Chapter 17

STATISTICAL PROCEDURES

To examine the efficacy of the Personal-Social Skills program, two groups of students (experimental and control) were compared on the two dependent measures, which were KB scores and CRS scores. For both the KB and CRS variables, the Analysis of Covariance (ANCOVA) was used to test the above-described hypothesis.

Chapter 18

KNOWLEDGE BATTERY (KB) ASSESSMENT

The Knowledge Battery was a standardized criterion-referenced instrument covering the three curriculum domains of Daily Living, Occupational Knowledge, and Personal-Social Skills. The Personal-Social skills segment contained questions for each of the targeted competencies with a total of 70 questions. Since the Knowledge Battery was a curriculum-based instrument, it is specifically designed to measure the instruction provided with the Personal-Social skills lessons. The results of the assessment were represented as a percentage.

Table 1. KB Descriptive Statistics

Descriptive Statistics

Dependent Variable: KB Posttest

Group	Mean	Std. Deviation	N
Control	57.55	21.717	20
Experimental	60.26	15.231	19
Total	58.87	18.644	39

COMPETENCY RATING SCALE (CRS)

The CRS required subjective judgments to be made on each of the Personal-Social skills subcompetencies. Students were rated on performance based upon the educator's observations, personal records or notes, and written or verbal reports from other personnel. Students were considered Not Competent (0), Partially Competent (1), Competent (2), or Not Rated.

Table 2. CRS Descriptive Statistics

Descriptive Statistics

Dependent Variable: CRS Postest

Group	Mean	Std. Deviation	N
Control	1.3530	.53183	20
Experimental	1.2674	.39353	19
Total	1.3113	.46547	39

Table 3. Pretest, Posttest, and Adjusted Means for Treatment Groups: Knowledge Battery

Group	Pretest	Posttest	Adjusted Posttest
Experimental	51.58	60.20	61.691
Control	55.15	57.55	56.193

Table 4. Pretest, Posttest, and Adjusted Means for Treatment Groups: Competency Rating Scale

Group	Pretest	Posttest	Adjusted Posttest
Experimental	.851	1.267	1.515
Control	1.356	1.353	1.118

Analyses of Data

Analyses of Knowledge Battery (KB) Assessment

The Analysis of Covariance (ANCOVA) statistical procedure examined the inequalities between the group means while taking into account the influence of a covariate. By comparing the means for the two groups, experimental and control, the linear associations between the posttest and pretest were given.

Table 5. KB ANCOVA: Analysis of Covariance Summary: Knowledge Battery

Source	Type III Sum of Squares	df	Mean Square	F	Sig.
Covariate (Pretest)	6308.163	1	6308.163	33.257	.000
Effect (Study)	291.065	1	291.065	1.535	.223
Error	6828.471	36	189.680		
Total	148378.000	39			
Corrected Total	13208.359	38			

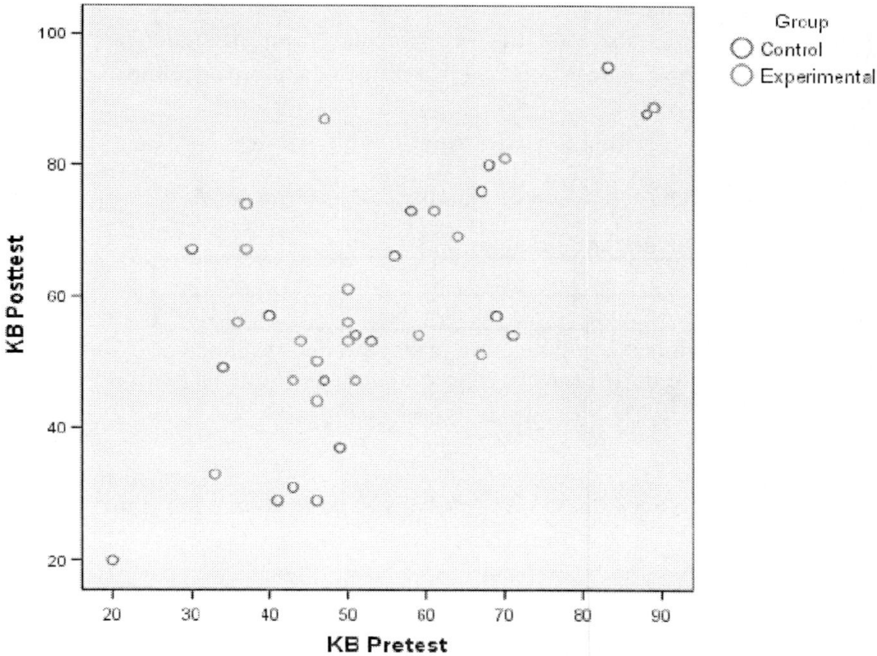

Graph 5. KB Pre and Posttest Results.

The effect of the covariate was significant, $F(1, 36) = 33.257$, $p < .0005$, indicating that the KB posttest and KB pretest were significantly correlated. However, the effect between groups was not significant F(1, 36) 1.535, p=.223. For this analysis, the equality-of-variances assumption was met, $F(1, 37) = 0.439$, $p = .512$ (Table 6). Furthermore, Graph 5 depicts the relationship between the KB posttest and KB pretest. The two variables had a positive relationship. However, no clear separation was seen between the two groups. In summary, the ANCOVA tells us that the two groups' means were not significantly different and the LCCE treatment did not have an effect.

ANALYSES OF COMPETENCY RATING SCALE (CRS)

The CRS pretest data shows that the means of CRS scores for the experimental and control groups were 0.851 and 1.356, respectively. For the CRS posttest, the means for the two groups were 1.267 and 1.353, respectively. Numerically, therefore, it appears that there was a sizable increase in the CRS score for the experimental group of students. However, the Analysis of Covariance statistical test reflected a more accurate analysis.

Table 6. CRS Equality of Variances

Levene's Test of Equality of Error Variances[a]

Dependent Variable: CRS Postest

F	df1	df2	Sig.
44.342	1	37	.000

Tests the null hypothesis that the error variance of the dependent variable is equal across groups.

a. Design: Intercept+crspre+study

Table 7. CRS ANCOVA: Analysis of Covariance Summary: Competency Rating Scale

Source	Type III Sum of Squares	df	Mean Square	F	Sig.
Covariate (Pretest)	6.922	1	6.922	200.971	.000
Effect (Study)	1.158	1	1.158	33.611	.000
Error	1.240	36	.034		
Total	75.292	39			
Corrected Total	8.233	38			

The effect of covariate was significant, $F(1, 36) = 200.971$, $p = .0005$. This indicated that the CRS posttest (response variable) and CRS pretest (covariate) were significantly correlated. The effect between groups was also significant, $F(1, 36) = 33.611$, $p < .0005$. The adjusted least-squares mean for the experimental group was higher ($M = 1.515$) than it was for the control group ($M = 1.118$). For this analysis, however, the equality-of-variances assumption was violated, $F(1, 37) = 44.342$, $p < .0005$ (Table 8). In conclusion, the experimental group's adjusted least-squares mean was higher than the control group's. This means that the treatment did have a positive effect however it was necessary to understand the ANCOVA violated the equality-of-variances assumption, and therefore interpretation as a positive result must be with caution.

Chapter 19

SUMMARY

In conclusion, both the KB and CRS data showed a slight increase in scores. However, when both the pre and posttest KB scores were analyzed using the ANCOVA, the test indicated that the intervention did not result in significantly higher test scores. On the other hand, the CRS ANCOVA test clearly indicated there was a significant increase in scores between the pre and posttest scores of the experimental group over the control group. Nevertheless, these results must be interpreted with caution due to the CRS violating the equality of variance assumption. Therefore, the hypothesis was rejected as the students in the experimental group, LCCE's Personal-Social Skills program, did not achieve significantly higher scores on the Knowledge Battery (KB) and Competency Rating Scale (CRS) than students in the control group, who did not participate in the program.

Chapter 20

EDUCATOR SURVEY

The educators completed the Communication Styles Checklist and the Curriculum Content Checklist which provided additional information regarding the rationale behind the results. Both educators agreed that any of the students' improvements were a result of the direct extensive instruction spent on the personal-social skills lessons and the immediacy in which the tests were given following the instructional intervention. Both educators expressed the belief that repetitive instruction on any subject would likely yield similar results. In addition, concern over whether or not students would retain information over time was addressed by both educators involved.

Chapter 21

SUMMARY AND DISCUSSION

The hypothesis stated that students in classes that utilize the LCCE's Personal-Social Skills program achieved significantly higher scores on the Knowledge Battery and Competency Rating Scale (CRS) than students who did not participate in the program. The results of the KB suggested that the means of the experimental group of students were not significantly different that the means of the control group. On the other hand, it was determined that the CRS variable for the experiment and control mean scores demonstrated some increase, while those of the control group showed nearly no change. It could be assumed that the LCCE program was successful in increasing the personal–social skills scores. However, it is essential to be cautious while interpreting this data as the ANCOVA test did violate the equality-of-variances assumption.

In conclusion, the results indicated that the research hypothesis was rejected; students participating in the experimental group did not show a greater increase in scores on the Knowledge Battery and Competency Rating Scale than the students who belonged to the control group. Furthermore, interviews with the participating instructors indicated that the experimental group would potentially demonstrate significantly higher scores if the personal-social skills curriculum was continued over an extended period of time and continuously reinforced.

However, the slight increase in scores suggested that with direct intervention, students with disabilities can exhibit improvement in specific areas. By reviewing the degree of change between the experimental and control group (posttest minus pretest) it was clear that there was a greater increase in scores within the experimental group. For the KB, the mean change scores for the control group were 2.40, compared to the mean change score of 8.68 for the experimental group. Similarly, on the CRS, the mean change score were 0.416 for the experimental group and -0.003 for the change group. These change scores clearly illustrated that although minimal, the intervention was successful in increasing the scores of the experimental group.

As a result of this slight increase in change scores within the experimental group, it can be assumed that over time a personal-social skills curriculum can have positive effects. Consequently, a functional curriculum supported by academics allows for students with intellectual disabilities to utilize functional skills that enabled them to live and work within their community. Nevertheless, the current trend is for students to be exposed to the general education curriculum, preventing students from receiving essential instruction in nonacademic areas such as personal-social skills. According to VDOE (2006-2007):

> Recognition that students with significant cognitive disabilities have instructional needs that are beyond the regular standards adopted by the general population is an accepted fact by researchers in the field of severe disabilities. However, NCLB and IDEA require that general grade level state standards be accessible for all students, including those with the most significant cognitive disabilities (p. 5).

Therefore, the curriculum utilized in the education of students with cognitive delays must include integrated life skills as well as an academic curriculum. One such vital life skill essential for students with intellectual disabilities to be exposed to was personal or social skills. The implementation of a specific personal or social skills program, such as LCCE, was essential in the development of social skills necessary for students to learn in order to function within their community.

SIMILAR STUDIES

Current studies within the field of special education that relate to this study center on students' participation and progress within the general education curriculum (Hager and Slocum, 2002). Many educators were seeking to determine if the standards-based reform was creating a curriculum for students with intellectual disabilities that was more academic, resulting in less time being spent on functional skills (Agran, Alper, and Wehmeyer, 2002).

Similar studies have been completed with regard to the LCCE curriculum and social skill integration with students with intellectual disabilities. The LCCE curriculum can be employed to increase the self-determination needs in youth with mild cognitive disabilities. This study focused on the four specific goals within the LCCE domains that specifically addressed self-determination: self-awareness, self-confidence, choice and decision-making skills, and goal attainment behaviors. "The LCCE offers today's educators a comprehensive and effective means for fulfilling their critical role in facilitating the development of self-determination in students with and without disabilities" (Wehmeyer, 1995, p. 165).

Similar studies utilizing the LCCE program compared the Occupational Guidance and Preparation domains' competencies and subcompetencies with specific data found on IEPs of high school students with learning disabilities (Schlegel, 1998). In another study, (O'Leary, 1991) the LCCE curriculum was employed as the curriculum framework to measure educational outcomes. The purpose of this study was to measure the most important educational outcomes perceived by parents, special educators, regular educators, and employers of students with intellectual disabilities. Results indicated that the "validation for the major curricular areas (domains) and competencies in the LCCE model is provided by parents, regular educators, and employers" (O'Leary, 1991, p. 1).

In addition to studies utilizing the LCCE curriculum, similar studies have been completed with the integration of social skills training with students who are mentally retarded. Defalco (1989) incorporated real-life probes to show that three specific social skills were acquired by three students with intellectual disabilities. This instruction reported that students were able to successfully generalize social skills into real-life situations through the use of both interventions: stimulus-control and response-consequences.

An additional study conducted by Quintana (2004) in social skills with students with intellectual disabilities involved a single subject study utilizing an A-B-A-B design and the implementation of a social skills training program addressing negative behaviors. Results indicated that there was a positive effect between the social skills training and the subject's behavior.

According to the Office on Special Education Rehabilitation Services (OSERS), current related research focused on the use of alternate assessments and their relationship with the general education curriculum and social skills training. Research conducted by Agran, Alper, & Wehmeyer (2002) focused on the federal mandates to assure access for all students and that it might not be beneficial for students with severe disabilities.

> We maintain that the ultimate goal of access to the general education curriculum for students with disabilities is successful and meaningful outcomes. We also agree with McDonnell, Thorson, and McQuivey's (2000) call for more research focused on how to embed a variety of social, functional academics, and transition skills within the ongoing activities and curriculum in the general education classroom (p. 130).

In addition, the researchers had teachers rank the importance of nine skill areas essential for facilitating access for students to the general education curriculum. Results indicated that social skills and communication skills were scored as the two most important skill areas. These results further indicated the need for a functional curriculum with social skills instruction.

APPLICATIONS

For students with intellectual disabilities, a functional curriculum supported by academics allows them to utilize functional skills that enabled them to live and work within their community. However, the current trend is for students to be exposed to the general education curriculum, preventing students from receiving essential instruction in nonacademic areas such as personal-social skills. The increase in scores of the Personal-Social skills curriculum indicated that long-term extensive instruction could be beneficial to continue to incorporate necessary functional life skills into the curriculum of students with intellectual disabilities.

In addition, a curriculum that addressed academics and life skills, such as the LCCE program, could be utilized to address other vital issues within the special education field. Current trends in special education reflect several issues: integration, participation in an outcomes-based assessment process, self-determination, functional life skills, and transitional services (Brolin, 1997). The LCCE curriculum contained considerable elements that relate to each of these movements. The utilization of LCCE's curriculum can have an influence on all of these issues.

The first trend of integration stems from the concept of normalization. "Normalization dictates that both the means and the ends of education for people with disabilities should be as normal as possible" (Hallahan &

Kauffman, 2000, p. 44). The drive towards integration has been instigated by the deinstitutionalization movement and the push for full inclusion. During the 1960s people with disabilities were slowly moved out of institutional settings into community placements. Likewise, inclusion advocates fought for the rights for students with disabilities to attend their neighborhood schools, placing the responsibility of education on the local educational systems. The utilization of the LCCE curriculum would assist in increasing students' social skills. As a result, students were more successful when integrated into regular education classes.

The second trend that the LCCE curriculum addressed was the use of outcomes-based education (OBE). OBE was based on the tenets that education should equip all students with the knowledge, skills, and competencies needed for mastery. OBE also established the conditions with schools that maximize the achievement and success for all students. The LCCE curriculum was an outcomes-based education system. "Many schools implementing LCCE have recognized this fact and have designated LCCE as their outcomes-based response to their state's and/or school district's mandate to implement the OBE approach" (Brolin, 1997, p. 3).

The third trend in special education was striving for students to learn to become self-determined. Self-determination was characterized by the attitudes within people that allow them to set goals for themselves and then take the initiative to meet these goals. The LCCE curriculum contained numerous strategies that work to increase students' self-determination. "The LCCE provides a comprehensive foundation upon which student instruction in self-determination can be accomplished and through which students can become more self-determined and involved in their educational process" (Brolin, 1997, p. 3).

In addition, there is a movement towards the utilization of functional skills and the need to blend academics with functional skills instruction within the school, home, and community settings. The functional skills addressed within the LCCE curriculum consist of independent living, social, communication, and vocational skills. Since the LCCE curriculum focused on 22 major functional skills, it provided a comprehensive background for delivering functional skills that will allow students with disabilities to function as productive members of their communities and as employees.

Finally, the mandate for transitional services has spurred a new movement. These services included postsecondary education, vocational training, integrated employment, continuing and adult education, adult services, independent living, and community participation. These services were mandates to be incorporated into the IEP with an emphasis on both employment and issues pertaining to the enhancement of students with disabilities' quality of life. This trend directly related to the need to have a vocational and life skills curriculum for students with intellectual disabilities. Transition is now mandated by IDEA to begin no later than age 16 and to be addressed within the IEP. The LCCE helps students to "learn and develop the critical skills they will need to be productive and successful upon making the transition from school to community life and work" (Brolin, 1997, p. 2).

Chapter 22

IMPLICATIONS FOR PRACTICE

One essential provision of *IDEA* was the mandate that every student found eligible for special education be provided with transition services. The LCCE enabled educators to fulfill this requirement through curriculum-based assessments and IEP documentation forms. As a result, the social skills of students with disabilities can easily be addressed and linked to students' Individualized Education Plan (IEP) goals and objectives. The CRS can be used in the development of IEPs as well as evaluations. "The cumulative average score resulting from a complete CRS rating can be used as one general index" (Brolin, 1997, p. 151). Furthermore, results of the LCCE Knowledge Battery can be an excellent source for documentation on the Present Level of Performance section of Eligibilities or annual IEPs.

The LCCE program has developed forms that allows for ease of integrating the curriculum into an IEP (See Appendix F). The LCCE Individualized Education Plan Forms allow educators to develop present levels of performance, goals, and objectives from the results of the CRS. "The LCCE IEP form could be used as the transition component and attached to the regular IEP form used by the school district" (Brolin, 1997, p.139).

Chapter 23

SIGNIFICANCE OF THE STUDY

By successfully incorporating a Personal-Social skills curriculum into a special education program for students with intellectual disabilities, other subpopulations could benefit. The concept would involve incorporating a social skills training into other populations such as students with learning disabilities, students with emotional disturbances, students in Alternative schools, students in General Education Degree (GED) programs, or even students who participate in English as a Second Language (ESL) programs.

In addition, general education teachers could become motivated to integrate universal life skill lessons, from LCCE, into core curriculum classes. An additional application of the LCCE curriculum would be to emphasize the incorporation of social skills training into other subgroups found within school settings. This would be an excellent opportunity to provide this form of instruction to students who are learning disabled or emotionally disturbed. Furthermore, social skills integration can be an excellent opportunity to incorporate state standards into lessons. The use of a program which incorporates social skills instruction with functional academics can provide instruction for a high school student which is practical, age appropriate, and easily linked to state specified Standards of Learning.

Finally, by determining the effectiveness of a social skills program for students with special needs, educators will be able to better serve students who are cognitively disabled. By implementing a successful program, school systems can address the personal and social needs. When students with special educational needs receive specific instruction on social skills, potential behavioral problems can also be reduced.

Chapter 24

LIMITATIONS OF THE STUDY

It was critical to understand the limits of the study being completed. These limits centered on the subjects as well as the time. First, the nature of working with students with mental disabilities was often inconsistent. It was often difficult to ascertain progress of students with intellectual disabilities as they frequently progress at slower rates and required additional time and instruction to grasp essential concepts. "Special education research, because of its complexity, may be the hardest of the hardest-to-do sciences. One feature of special education research that makes it more complex is the variability of the participants" (Odom et al, 2005, p. 139).

Furthermore, the demographics represented were limited with regard to race and ethnicity. Augusta County Schools are located in a rural community with less than one percent of the students being African-American and Hispanic. This limitation made it difficult to generalize the findings of the study to the general population. In addition, the small sample size could be viewed as a potential limitation. Since there were only 39 students participating in the study, results of the findings could be difficult to relate to the population of special education students.

Along the same lines as the limitations that the population might impose, the time constraints of the study could also be an indicator affecting the outcomes. The study occurred over the course of seven weeks. The LCCE curriculum was a comprehensive curriculum that could be utilized over the middle or high school careers of students with intellectual disabilities. The Personal-Social domain should be incorporated into instruction repeatedly before students could show progress. As a result, the degree of improvement found within a seven week study was minimal.

Chapter 25

RECOMMENDATIONS FOR FURTHER RESEARCH

This study created numerous opportunities for further research. First, this study could be expanded to include a larger population of students participating.

Furthermore, it would be beneficial to complete a longitudinal study to determine the degree of students' improvements over the course of middle and high school as instruction is provided throughout their education. Finally, further studies resulting from this research could revolve around incorporating any portion of the LCCE curriculum into various populations such as students with learning disabilities or emotional disabilities.

REFERENCES

American Association on Mental Retardation. (2002). *The definition of mental retardation*. Available online from: http://www.aamr.org.

Agran, M., Alper, S., & Wehmeyer, M. (2002). Access to the general curriculum for students with significant disabilities: What it means to teachers. *Education and Training in Mental Retardation and Developmental Disabilities*, 37(2), 123-133.

Ahlgrim-Delzell, L., Algozzine, R., Browder, D., Flowers, C., Karvonen, M., Spooner, F. (2004). The alignment of alternate assessment content with academic and functional curricula. *Journal of Special Education*, 37.

Bertone, L., Boyle, J., Mitchel, J., & Smith, J. (1999). Improving pro-social behavior through social skills instruction. *U.S. Department of Education.*

Black, R. & Salas, B., (2001). Forty years of progress: Where have we been? Where are we now? *Annual Meeting of the American Association on Mental Retardation.*

Brolin, D. (1997). *Life centered career education*. The Council for Exceptional Children.

Browder, D.M., & Cooper-Duffy, K. (2003).Evidence-based practices for students with severe disabilities and the requirement for accountability in "No Child Left Behind". *The Journal of Special Education*, 37, 3, 157-163.

Bruckerhoff, C. (1996). Who knows what? *Curriculum research and evaluation.*

Cartledge, G. & Kiarie, M. (2001). Learning social skills through literature for children and adolescents. *Teaching Exceptional Children*, 34, 2, 40-47.

Cernosia, A. (2005). The reauthorization of IDEA and significant judicial decisions. *California Department of Education Sponsored Training.*

Council for Exceptional Children (CEC). (2003). No Child Left Behind Act of 2001: implications for special education policy and practice. *Council for Exceptional Children.*

Cuskelly, M. (2004). The evolving construct of intellectual disability: is everything old new again? *International Journal of Disability, Development and Education,* 51, 1.

deBettencourt, L. (2002). Understanding the differences between Section 504 and ADA. *Teaching Exceptional Children, 34*, 3, 16-23.

de Bildt, A., Serra, M., Luteijn, E., Kraijer, D., Sytema, S., & Minderaa, R. (2005). Social skills in children with intellectual disabilities with and without autism. *Journal of Intellectual Disability Research, 49*, 5, 317-328.

Defalco, G.A., (1989).Generalized use of social skills in natural settings by people with mental retardation. Available: *DAI, 51,* no. 04B (1989): p. 2057.

DeWeaver, K. & Kropf, N. (1992). Persons with mental retardation: A forgotten minority in education. *Journal of Social Work Education,* 28, 1, 36-47.

Ford, A., Schnorr, R., Meyer, L., Davern, L., Black, J., Dempsey, P. (1989). *The Syracuse community referenced curriculum guide: for students with moderate and severe disabilities.* Baltimore, MD: Brookes Publishing:

Gartin, B. & Murdick, N. (2004). IDEA 2004: The IEP. *Remedial and SpecialEducation, 26*, 6, 327-331.

Hallahan, D. & Kauffman, J. (2000). *Exceptional learners: introduction to special education.* Boston: Allyn & Bacon.

Kearsley, G. (2006). Social Learning Theory (A. Bandura). *Exploration in Learning & Instruction: The theory into practice database.* Available online from:http://tip.psychology.org/bandura.html

Kolb, S. & Hanley-Maxwell, C. (2003). Critical social skills for adolescents with high incidence disabilities: parental perspectives. *Council for Exceptional Children*, 69, 2, 163-179.

Matson, J., Mayville, E., Lott, J., Bielecki, J., & Logan, R. (2003). A comparison of social and adaptive functioning in persons with psychosis, autism, and severe or profound mental retardation. *Journal of Developmental and Physical Disabilities,* 15, 1.

Menta Group. (2006). *Clinical services model. Special Education Services.* Available online: www.mentagroup.com.

NASET. (2006). Landmark cases in special education. *National Association of Special Education Teachers*. www.naset.org/landmarkcases.0.html

National Center on Educational Outcomes. (2005). Available online: *http://education.umn.edu/NCEO*

Odom, S., Brantlinger, E., Gersten, R., Horner, R., Thompson, B., Harris, K. (2005). Research in special education: Scientific methods and evidence-based practices. *Council for Exceptional Children*, 71, 2, 137-148.

O'Leary, E.E., (1991). Consensual validation of educational outcomes for high school students with mild disabilities. Available: *DAI, 52,* no. 07A (1991): p. 2503.

Paige, R. (2004) A guide to education and *No Child Left Behind. U.S. Department of Education*. Available online: www.ed.gov.

Paraschiv, I. & Oiley, G. (1999). Generalization of social skills: Strategies and results of a training program in problem solving skills. *U.S. Department of Education*

Payne, J. & Patton, J. (1981). *Mental Retardation*. Charles E. Merrill Publishing Co.: Columbus.

Quintana, A. (2004). Efficacy of a social skills training procedure used on a child having moderate mental retardation. Available: *MAI, 43*, no. 03 (2004): p. 663.

Rea, P. & Davis-Dorsey, J. (2004). ADA in the public school setting. *Journal of Disability Policy Studies*, 15, 2, 66-69.

Robinson, et al. (1989). *Best practices in mild mental disabilities*. The Division on Mental Retardation of the Council for Exceptional Children.

Schlegel, B.J. (1998). A comparison of the life-centered career education model to the individual transition plans of high school students with learning disabilities. Available: *MAI, 37*, no. 01 (1998): 0051.

Shriner, J.G. (2000). Legal perspectives on school outcome assessment for students with disabilities. *Journal of Special Education*, 33, 4, 232-240.

Smith, T. (2001). Section 504, the ADA, and Public Schools. *Remedial & Special Education*. 6, 335-344.

Sutton, J. (1993). *Special education: A biblical approach* South Carolina: Hidden Treasure.

Thomas, G. (1996). *Teaching students with metal retardation: a life goal curriculum approach*. Prentice-Hall, Inc.: New Jersey.

VDOE (2006-2007). *Virginia Alternate Assessment Program (VAAP) Instructional Manual: A teacher resource for the aligned standards of learning*. Division of Special Education Instructional Services.

Wehmeyer, M. (1995). A career education approach: self-determination for youth with mild cognitive disabilities. *Intervention in School & Clinic*, 30, 3, 157-164.

Wehmeyer, M., Lance, G., & Bashinski, S. (2002). Promoting access to the general education curriculum for students with mental retardation: A multi-level model. *Education and Training in Mental Retardation and Developmental Disabilities,* 37, 3, 223-234.

Yell, M. & Katsiyannis, A. (2004). Placing students with disabilities in inclusive settings: Legal guardians and preferred practices. *Preventing School Failure*, Fall

INDEX

A

B

C

D

E

F

G

H

I

L

M

N

O

P

Q

R

S

T

V

W

Y